First World War
and Army of Occupation
War Diary
France, Belgium and Germany

9 DIVISION
2 Lowland Brigades
King's Own Scottish Borderers
6th Battalion.
1 April 1919 - 31 August 1919

WO95/1776/7

Published by

The Naval & Military Press Ltd

Unit 10 Ridgewood Industrial Park,
Uckfield, East Sussex,
TN22 5QE England
Tel: +44 (0) 1825 749494

www.naval-military-press.com
www.nmarchive.com

This diary has been reprinted in facsimile from the original. Any imperfections are inevitably reproduced and the quality may fall short of modern type and cartographic standards.

© **Crown Copyright**
Images reproduced by permission of The National Archives, London, England, 2015.

Contents

Document type	Place/Title	Date From	Date To
Heading	Highland (9) Division 2nd Highland Bde 6th K O S B 1919 Apr-1919 Oct From 27 Bde 9 Div		
War Diary	Mulheim	01/04/1919	06/04/1919
War Diary	Wald	07/04/1919	30/04/1919
War Diary	Wald Germany	01/05/1919	16/05/1919
War Diary	Wald	17/05/1919	09/07/1919
War Diary	Nieder-Aussem	10/07/1919	13/08/1919
War Diary	Duren	14/08/1919	31/08/1919

HIGHLAND (9) DIVISION

2nd HIGHLAND BDE

6th K.O.S.B

1919 APR — 1919 OCT

From 27 BDE 9 DIV

WAR DIARY or INTELLIGENCE SUMMARY.

Army Form C. 2118.

6th K.O.S. Borderers

Place	Date	Hour	Summary of Events and Information	Remarks and references to Appendices
Mulheim	Apl 1	9-10 10-12	Arms Platoon Drill. Recreational Training. Lecture on "Demobilisation" etc. Enlistment by Lt. Hallam Border Regt.	
do	2	9-12	Coy Platoon & Squad Drill. Recreational Training	
do	3	9-2.30	Lieut. Col. J. S. Hackney DSO MC assumed command of the Battalion	
do	4	9-11	Cleaning up. Commanding Officer inspected billets. Recreational Training	
do	5	—	Two Coys moved to Wald. Two boys on Coy Drill & Rec Training.	
do	6	9-12	Recreational Training. Squad Drill. Handling of arms	
Wald	7	—	Two Coys + HQ left for Wald. Relieved by 16th KSLI 9.	
do	8	—	Cleaning of billets required. Commanding. Battalion Baths	
do	9	8.30-12.30	Two Coys commenced training — Physical, Musketry, Field. Ceremonial 1st wk. 2nd day.	
do	10	8.30-12.30	Training Programme continued	
do	11	8.30-11	Cleaning up. Billet inspection. Health Inspector Govats warned at Retreat.	
do	12	10.25	Divine Service. Pres. C. of E & R. Cs. Voluntary Service in evening	
do	13	8.30-12.30	Training as per programme. Education classes commenced	
do	14	8.30-12.30	Training. Battalion Baths	
do	15	8.30-12.30	Rapid Loading in Musketry. Field Training. Baths for Generals	
do	16	8.30-12.30	Training as per programme. Coy Route March. Lecture by ADMS "Dangers & Prev. of VD"	
do	17	8.30-12	Recreational Field Training. Afternoon Football. 6th KOSB v 11th Royal Scots	

Army Form C. 2118.

WAR DIARY
or
INTELLIGENCE SUMMARY.
(Erase heading not required.)

Instructions regarding War Diaries and Intelligence
Summaries are contained in F. S. Regs., Part II.
and the Staff Manual respectively. Title pages
will be prepared in manuscript.

Place	Date	Hour	Summary of Events and Information	Remarks and references to Appendices
Wald	18 Apl	8.30-12.30	Training as per programme. Football afternoon:- Officers v Batt. Sergeants	
"	19 "	10.25	Divine Service. Pres. 6 Off. rR.B.	
"	20 "		Easter Monday observed as Battalion Holiday.	
"	21 "		Training as per programme. Batt. Inoculation.	
"	22 "	8.30-12.30	Specialist Training. Education Lewis Gun Instruction	
"	23 "	8.30	Route March by Coys. WALD - HOLZ. Officers not on duty instr in L. Gun by L/C Officers.	
"	24 "	8.30-12.30	Field Training. Recreational Training. Inter-Coy Football Match	
"	25 "	8.30	Route March by Coy. Education Classes.	
"	26 "	9.30	Commanding Officers inspection of draft. 5/6th R.S. relieved at KLUSE vc by 6th KOSB	
"	27 "	10.25	Divine Service. Pres. 6 Offs r RB. Officers Football Match in afternoon	
"	28 "	8.30-12.30	Field Training. Recreational Training.	
"	29 "	9-12.30	Education. Recreational Training. Field Training	
"	30th	8.30-12.30	Field Training. Batt. Baths. Recreational Training.	
"	Apl.			

1st May 1919

F.S. Thackeray
Lieut-Col.
Commanding 6th K.O.S.Bors.

6th King's Own Scottish Borderers

WAR DIARY
or
INTELLIGENCE SUMMARY.
(Erase heading not required.)

Instructions regarding War Diaries and Intelligence Summaries are contained in F.S. Regs., Part II. and the Staff Manual respectively. Title pages will be prepared in manuscript.

Army Form C. 2118.

H.Q.
2nd Lowland Bde.

Place	Date	Hour	Summary of Events and Information	Remarks and references to Appendices
Wald, Germany.	1/5/19	8.30-9.30	Company Recreational Training.	
"	2 "	9-12	Education Classes. Recreational Training. Football inter Coy.	
"	3 "	9-12	Coy. Route March. WALD-HOLZ-BAVERT-WALD. Judging Dist. Training. Recreational Training afternoon.	
"	4 "	10.15	Divine Service. Pres. 6. off's + R.O's	
"	5 "	8.30-9.30	Field Training. Recreational Training afternoon.	
"	6 "	9-12	Education Classes. Recreational Training. Baths. Lecture by Lt. Graham on "Intelligence"	
"	7 "	8.30-9.30	Field Training. Recreational Training. Football 6th K.O.S.B. v Bde. MMG	
"	8 "	9-12	Education Classes. R.E's Instruction Class commenced.	
"	9 "	8.30	Coys. relieved two coys. at outposts in Route March fashion.	
"	10 "	8.30-11.30	Education Classes. Kit Inspection 11.30-12.30. Inter Coy. Football.	
"	11 "	10.15	Divine Service. Pres. Boff's + R.Os. Voluntary Service in Sa. Ch. Hut in evening.	
"	12 "	8.30-12.30	Education Classes. Kit Inspection.	
"	13 "	8.30-12.30	Field Training. Recreational Training. Football. Baths.	
"	14 "	8.30-12.30	Coy. Route March with Pipe Band.	
"	15 "	8.30-2.30	Company Training. Gas. Field Training.	
"	16 "	9-12.30	Education Classes. 1.30-4.30 Recreational Training.	

Army Form C. 2118.

WAR DIARY
or
INTELLIGENCE SUMMARY.
(Erase heading not required.)

Instructions regarding War Diaries and Intelligence Summaries are contained in F.S. Regs., Part II. and the Staff Manual respectively. Title pages will be prepared in manuscript.

Place	Date	Hour	Summary of Events and Information	Remarks and references to Appendices
Wald	May 17	8.45-12	Lecture by Lt. Col. Eysham. Subject "The Fallacies of Bolshevism". Solingen	
" "	18	10.35	Divine Service. Bn. B. of 8. r.B. Voluntary Service 6.30.	
" "	19	8.30-12.30	Field Training. Recreational Training.	
" "	20	6.30	Relief of Outposts. Guards mounted 17.00 hrs in lieu of 19.30.	
" "	21	8.30-12.30	Coy. Training. Recreational Training. Solingen Concert Party. Sec. 6th Btn.	
" "	22	" "	Coy & Recreational Training. Football Match. 6th SCOLB v 2nd Lowl M.B.	
" "	23	" "	Field Training. Route March with Pipe Band. Recreation.	
" "	24	" "	Coy. Training. Education Classes. Recreation	
" "	25	10.35	Divine Service. Bn. B. of 8. r.B. Voluntary Service Scottish Br. Ch.	
" "	26	8.30-12.30	Field Training. Recreation. Battalion Baths.	
" "	27	8.30-12.30	Coy. Training. Baths. Recreational Training.	
" "	28	8.30-12.30	Field Training & Recreation. Open Air Swimming Baths.	
" "	29	8.30-12.30	Coy. Route March cancelled. Coy. standing to in Billets	
" "	30	8.30-12.30	Training in Coy. Recreation. Education. Football Match.	
" "	31	9-12	C.O's inspection of Billets. M.O. Health Inspection. Football Match. Officers v Sergts.	

F S Anderson

6th KOSB
2nd Line Bn
Low TM

Army Form C. 2118.

WAR DIARY
or
INTELLIGENCE SUMMARY.
(Erase heading not required.)

Instructions regarding War Diaries and Intelligence Summaries are contained in F. S. Regs., Part II. and the Staff Manual respectively. Title pages will be prepared in manuscript.

Place	Date	Hour	Summary of Events and Information	Remarks and references to Appendices
Wald.	1.	—	Divine Services:- Kit. 08·00. Presbyterans 10·25. R of Es 11·30.	
—	2.	—	08·30 to 12·45:- Coy. Comndr Inspection, Musketry, Arm Drill, Moral Discipline, Foot Order Drill, Platoon Drill, P.F.B.F. List.	
—	3.	—	08·30 to 09·30:- Kit Inspection. 09·30 to 12·30:- Education.	
—	4.	—	08·30 to 12·30:- Buckerhote Range. Relig. Bucklorf, Solingen Square. K. 7° 89.	
—	5.	—	08·30 to 12·30:- Buckerhote Range. Relig. Bucklorf, Solingen Square. K. 7° 89.	
—	6.	—	08·30 to 09·30:- Company Inspection. 09·30 to 12·30:- F.T. + B.F. 10·45 to 12·45:- Education.	
—	7.	—	07·30 to 09·00:- Physical Training. 09·00 to 10·00:- Medical Inspection. 10·00 to 12·45:- Medical Inspection.	
—	8.	—	Divine Services:- Presbyterians 10·25. R of Es 11·15.	
—	9.	—	08·30 to 12·45:- Coy. Comndr Inspn. Musketry, March to Brickerhote Rifle Practice. P.F.B.F. List Drill, Foot Law Drill, Ceremonial Drill (Pipe Band)	
—	10.	—	08·30 to 12·30:- Buckerhote Range. Relig. Bucklorf, Solingen Square. K. 7° 89.	
—	11.	—	08·30 to 12·30:- Buckerhote Range. Relig. Bucklorf, Solingen Square. K. 7° 89.	
—	12.	—	08·30 to 09·30:- Musketry. Revision Lecture. 09·30 to 12·30:- Education.	
—	13.	—	08·30 to 09·45:- Coy. Inspection. 08·45 to 09·30:- Kit Inspection. 09·30 to 10·30. P.T. + B.F. 10·45 to 12·45:- Education.	
—	14.	—	08·30 to 09·30:- Ref. Bombing. 09·30 to 10·00:- Medical Inspection. 10·00 to 12·45:- Education.	
—	15.	—	Divine Services:- C of E. 09·30. Presbyterans 10·25. R.C. 11·15.	
—	16.	—	08·30 to 12·45:- March to Brickerhote. Cooking Application, Kubis Practice in Rabid Loading 10 Rds Standard Test	

Army Form C. 2118.

WAR DIARY
or
INTELLIGENCE SUMMARY.
(Erase heading not required.)

Instructions regarding War Diaries and Intelligence Summaries are contained in F. S. Regs. Part II. and the Staff Manual respectively. Title pages will be prepared in manuscript.

Place	Date	Hour	Summary of Events and Information	Remarks and references to Appendices
Wald	17	—	08·30 to 12·45. Education.	
—	18	—	08·30 to 12·30. Bruchstottenlange, Bliss, Dusseldorf-Solingen-Square K 189.	
—	19	—	08·30 to 09·30. Musketry, Winsor Lecture. 09·30 to 12·30. Education	
—	20	—	08·30 to 10·30. Coy Inspection. 08·45 to 09·30. Kit Inspection. 09·30 to 10·30. PT·B·F. 10·15 to 12·45. Education	
—	21	—	08·30 to 12·30. Kit Inspection, Medical Inspection, March to Range (Rile Range) Lecture, Rifle Running, Arm Drills, March back.	
—	22	—	Divine Services. C. of E. 09·45. Presbyterians 10·30. RC. 11·30	
—	23	—	08·30 to 09·30. Coy Commdt. inspect. 09·30 to 12·30. Education	
—	24	—	08·30 to 12·30. Advance Guard, All U. formations, Coy in attack. Musketry, Coy drill, Sect Ouevr. PT·BF·Bayoneting	
—	25	—	08·30 to 9·30. Gas Chamber. 09·30 to 12·30. Education	
—	26	—	08·30 to 12·30. Musketry, 30 yds Range Advance Guard, Artillery Formations, Coy in attack. N° 2 Training, Arts.	
—	27	—	08·30 to 10·30. Kit Medical Inspection — Education.	
—	28	—	08·30 to 12·30. Bruchstotten Range, Bliss, three practices, 30 yds range.	
—	29	—	Divine Services. C. of E. 10·00. Presbyterians 10·25. RC. 11·15	
—	30	—	08·30 to 09·00. Coy Commdt Inspection. 09·00 to 10·00. Commanding Officer's Inspection. 10·00 to 12·30. Drill, PT·BF·Musketry etc.	

F. M. ——
Lt.-Colonel.
Commanding 6th K.O. Scot. Bord.

6 Mosbo. July 1919. Army Form C. 2118.

WAR DIARY
or
INTELLIGENCE SUMMARY.
(Erase heading not required.)

5.
Whets

Place	Date	Hour	Summary of Events and Information	Remarks and references to Appendices
Wald	1	08-30 to 09-30	Company Commanders Drabroot - 10-00 to 12-30 - Instruction	
"	2	08-30 to 12-30	Bruckotten Range. Illigo.	
"	3	08-30 to 12-30	Education. Lieut. Col. J.S. Hackney DSO MC relinquished command of the Battn.	
"	4		General Holiday - (Empire Day) Lieut. Colonel E.B. Jackson DSO assumed command of the Battn.	
"	5	08-30 to 12-30	Bruckotten Range - Illigo.	
"	6		Divine Services - Presbyterians at 10-25 C of E. at 10-30. R.C. at 11-15 A.M.	
"	7	08-30 to 09-30	Company Spring (Drill Musketry) 09-30 to 10-30 - Instruction.	
"	8		Packing of Stores and cleaning of Billets	
"	9		Battalion Move to Nieder Aussem.	
Nieder Aussem	10		Companies at Disposal of Company Commanders.	
"	11	09-30 to 11-30	Musketry, Jork Change - 09-30 to 11-30 - Instruction.	
"	12	09-30 to 11-30	Route March (Drill Dress) - 09-30 to 11-30 - Musketry, 30 Yds Range.	
"	13		Divine Service - Presbyterians at 09-30 (Huissen) R.C at 09-30 (Nieder Aussem) C of E 15 (Nr. Aussen)	
"	14	08-30 to 09-30	Company Training - 09-30 to 12-30 - Instruction	
"	15	08-30 to 09-30	Company Training - 09-30 to 12-30 - Combined in attack (Front 3 RWF Lly Sq 25/56)	
"	16	08-30 to 12-30	Battalion Route March.	

WAR DIARY or INTELLIGENCE SUMMARY

Army Form C. 2118.

(Erase heading not required.)

Instructions regarding War Diaries and Intelligence Summaries are contained in F. S. Regs., Part II. and the Staff Manual respectively. Title pages will be prepared in manuscript.

Place	Date	Hour	Summary of Events and Information	Remarks and references to Appendices
Nieder-Anwen	17	08·30 to 09·30	Company Training – 09·30 to 13·30 – 30 Yds. Range.	
"	18	08·30 to 09·30	Company Training – 09·30 to 12·30 Rifle Parade	
"	19		General Holiday – Peace Day	
"	20		Divine Service – Religious Service at 10·30 (R.C.) at 09·00 (Nieder-Anwen) 07·30 (Ober-Anwen)	
"	21	09·00 to 09·45	Company Training – 10·00 to 12·30 – Education	
"	22	09·30 to 10·30	Commanding Officer's Parade – 11·00 to 12·30 – Company Training	
"	23	09·00 to 09·45	Miniature Range – 10·00 to 12·30 – Education	
"	24	09·00 to 09·40	Coy Company Training – 10·00 to 14·00 – Lecture (War Savings) 14·15 to 17·30 – Brigade	
"	25	09·00 to 09·45	Company Training – 10·00 to 12·30 – Education	
"	26	09·00 to 12·30	Commanding Officer's Inspection of Kits and Billets.	
"	27		Divine Services – Presbyterian at 1–·15 (Julich) RC's at 09·30 (Nieder-Anwen) 07·00 (Ober-Anwen)	
"	28	09·00 to 09·45	Company Training – 10·00 to 12·30 – Education	
"	29	09·00 to 09·45	Miniature Range – 10·00 to 12·30 – Company attack (3 Btns E July 5 556)	
"	30	09·00 to 09·40	Co Company to Baths – 10·00 to 12·30 – Education	
"	31	09·30 to 10·30	Commanding Officer's Parade – 11·00 to 12·30 – Company Training	

S. Sutton
Lt-Colonel.
Commanding 6th K. O. Sco. Bord.

WAR DIARY
or
INTELLIGENCE SUMMARY.
(Erase heading not required.)

Army Form C. 2118.

6th KOSB Bn
August

Place	Date	Hour	Summary of Events and Information	Remarks and references to Appendices
Not Known	1	09.30 to 10.30	Commanding Officers Inspection. Coy. Training. Cricket Match	Inter Coy Cricket Match
"	2	10.30 to 12.30	Att v Batt. Inspection. Coy. Cricket Match	
"	3	11.15	Presbyterian or R.C. Divine Service. Football Match Officers v Sgts.	
"	4		Bank Holiday. Battalion Sports. Concert in evening	
"	5	10.00	Lecture on Umba on Pallets. Football Cricket Matches	
"	6	08.30 to 12.30	Company Training. Cricket Match 5/10th Batt v 6th KOSB	
"	7	09.30	Commanding Officers Parade. Coy. Cricket Match. Baths.	
"	8	08.30 to 09.30	Company Training. Ing of War Practice. Coy. Cricket Match. 9 Oth Boy 1.6 v 6th KOSB	
"	9	10-12.30	Battalion Inspection. Coy. Cricket Football Matches.	
"	10	10.15	Divine Service. Coy v Att. Coy. Cricket Football Matches.	
"	11	08.30 to 12.30	Company Training. Ing of War. Three Country Running Practice	
"	12	09.30	Commanding Officers Parade	
"	13	09.00	Battalion Move to Dinner	
Dinner	14	08.30 to 12.30	Clearing up & settling down in new Billets.	
"	15	09.00	L.O.U. Inspection of Billets. Company Training. Major Aw Robinson Wounded Went	
"	16	08.30 to 12.30	Company Training. Ing of War Practice. Sports Conference. IV Corps Searchlight Tattoo	

Aw Robinson. Major
for Lt-Colonel
Commanding 6th K.O. Sco. Bord

Army Form C. 2118.

WAR DIARY
or
INTELLIGENCE SUMMARY.
(Erase heading not required)

Instructions regarding War Diaries and Intelligence Summaries are contained in F. S. Regs., Part II. and the Staff Manual respectively. Title pages will be prepared in manuscript.

Place	Date	Hour	Summary of Events and Information	Remarks and references to Appendices
Lucues	17	10.15	Divine Service Presbyterian R.C.	
-"-	18	08.30	Company Training. Medical Inspection	
-"-	19	09.30	Battalion Baths. Company Training	
-"-	20	08.30	Company Commanders Camp Inspection	
-"-	21	10.00	G.O.C. Inspection Division. Marching Order, Two Days Kit Inspection	
-"-	22	08.30	Company Training. Bino Country Survey	
-"-	23	05.30	Re-arrangement of Billets by Companies	
-"-	24	10.00	Divine Service Presbyterian R.C.	
-"-	25	08.30	Company Training. Battalion Baths	
-"-	26	09.30	Battalion Route March.	
-"-	27	06.30	Company Training. Inter Coy Football Match	
-"-	28	09.20	Commanding Officers Church Parade	
-"-	29	08.30	Company Training. Boxing Practice	
-"-	30	10.00 to 12.30	Commanding Officers Kit Inspection	
-"-	31	10.00	Divine Service Pres. R.C. Cricket Match IV Corps HQ. v 2nd R. Rifle	

AM Johnson Major for Lt-Colonel
Commanding 6th K. O. Scot. Bord.

www.ingramcontent.com/pod-product-compliance
Lightning Source LLC
Chambersburg PA
CBHW081518160426
43193CB00014B/2727